FOSTER CARE AND ADOPTION

D1301265

BY
MARGARET O.
HYDE

FOSTER CARE AND ADOPTION

A GROLIER COMPANY

FRANKLIN WATTS
New York|London|Toronto|Sydney
1982

Library of Congress Cataloging in Publication Data

Hyde, Margaret Oldroyd, 1917–
Foster care and adoption.

Bibliography: p.
Includes index.
Summary: Examines the foster home care system
which enables children from troubled families to
be placed temporarily in other authorized homes.
Includes a brief discussion of adoption.
1. Foster home care—Juvenile literature.
2. Adoption—Juvenile literature.
[1. Foster home care.   2. Adoption]   I. Title.
HV875.H93   1982   362.7'33'0973   81-21971
ISBN 0-531-04403-3   AACR2

CONTENTS

CHAPTER

1

DOES ANYONE CARE?

Late one afternoon, four children are waiting at the emergency shelter of their community's child welfare office. For a variety of reasons, they cannot live at home with their own parents, and now they are waiting to be placed in foster homes.

Social workers were alerted to the case of 4-year-old Janie when a neighbor called to report that the little girl was often hungry. This morning, at Janie's house, they found her sleeping naked, without sheets or blankets, in a cold room. When a social worker questioned her about the child's condition, Janie's mother expressed relief at the idea of placing the girl with a foster family. "She was always whining or crying and getting on my nerves," complained the woman. "I didn't want her in the first place."

The caseworker for this neglected child will begin at once to search for a home that will provide long-term foster care. Efforts will also be made to help the mother learn to be a better parent, but if she cannot be helped, Janie will be a candidate for adoption.

A second child, Tony, arrived at the shelter yesterday, and he wants very much to go home. His mother also wants him back, and the social worker on the case is looking for a temporary homemaker to help her through an emotional crisis. Tony's father died just two months ago, and his mother, who was very much disturbed by the sudden death, began drinking heavily. She was not caring for her son properly, and the school authorities became concerned about the child's physical condition. They asked a social agency to investigate the situation. The agency found that the mother was having a difficult time and referred her to a local mental health clinic for counseling. If she responds well to the counseling and if other community services, such as a temporary homemaker, are available to her, Tony may return home in a few days. Without this kind of help, however, he could become one of the many foster children who are shuffled from home to home.

Pete was one of those who never went back to his parents' home. Now, after eight years, he is waiting for a new set of foster parents. He has just come from a home where he fought with the other foster children, disobeyed the rules, and was so disruptive that the parents refused to keep him another day. Finding a home for 13-year-old Pete will not be as easy as placing a younger, less difficult child.

The most recent arrival at the shelter is 3-year-old Sam. He is here because his mother had to go to the hospital for an emergency operation. She did not know anyone who could keep her son, so her doctor is helping to arrange for foster care through the child welfare bureau. While his mother is in the hospital, Sam may be placed in a home where the parents have been trained by an agency to care for foster children, or he may be placed with a family that has applied for a foster child but has no experience with the special problems that may arise. What happens to Sam will depend on the particular community and the kind of foster care that is available at the time.

Unlike many of the children who pass through the emergency shelter, Sam stands a good chance of being back home with his mother in just a few weeks. But suppose his mother remains unable to care for him for a longer time than she expects. Will the organizations that make up the foster care system help to reunite the family as quickly as possible?

[3]

If Sam's mother should die, will the child be made available for adoption by one of the many families who are searching for a 3 year old? Or will he stay indefinitely in foster care because the system is plagued with inadequate social services, ineffectual laws, and court systems that are unable or unwilling to put the needs of the child first?

FOSTER CARE—AN OVERVIEW

Foster care may be defined as any situation in which children live with people who act as substitute parents. Today's public child care system was originally designed to provide temporary arrangements for children who were abused, unwanted, or orphaned. These and many other conditions continue to cause children to leave the homes of their natural, or biological, parents to become part of the foster care systems run by cities, states, and private agencies.

As the example of a typical child welfare shelter illustrates, children from infants to adolescents are caught up in the foster care system. They are brought to the attention of child care agencies, both public and private, by a wide variety of methods. Some children go into foster care after being involved with juvenile court, and others because neighbors report neglect and abuse. Sometimes parents voluntarily place their children in foster care because of illness or a family crisis. Or agencies may learn of children whose parents have deserted them altogether.

The reasons for being placed away from their own families may vary greatly, but every child going into foster care experiences a dramatic, stressful change. The emotional pain may be long-lasting and very deep, because the consistent support and nurturing each child needs is missing from the lives of those who are shifted from one foster home to another.

Tragically, no one knows the exact number of children in care, but it is thought to be more than half a million. It is estimated that in the United States, one child in two hundred is living in a foster home, and some people believe that more than half of them have been in foster care for at least two

[4]

years. According to recent reports, it is probable that the average foster child has been in the public child care system approximately eight years and has lived in three different homes. For a child, eight years is a very long time. It is roughly 45 percent of a child's life before adulthood—that is the same as eighteen years in the life of a 40-year-old person.

Long-term foster care is especially sad when one considers that many children who become "lost" in the system could be returned to their homes or be placed in permanent homes through adoption. Billy's case illustrates what has been happening to many children in foster care. He was placed in a foster home when he was 4 years old, after his unemployed father had taken his frustrations out on the boy by beating him. This incident of child abuse was reported by a neighbor, and the county took custody of Billy for a six-month period. During this time some efforts were made to help the father learn to express his anger in more acceptable ways, in preparation for Billy's return. But before the six months went by, Billy's mother died, and his father grew very disturbed. Billy stayed with his foster parents.

During the next ten years, Billy lived in five foster homes and lost all contact with his emotionally disturbed father. He left the first home because it was only licensed to care for children up to the age of 6. The second home was one that cares for children for only short periods of time, and Billy soon learned that he would be moving to another family when one could be found. The little boy who had been happy in his first foster home now began to feel unwanted and frightened. In the third home, Billy was placed with parents who had three children of their own. Billy was their first foster child. He had outbursts of jealousy against the other children, and his behavior became so aggressive that these foster parents could not control him. They asked to have him removed from their home.

Billy entered the fourth foster home at the age of 9. By this time he had been in four different schools. He had been uprooted so often that it was not surprising that his emotional and intellectual development was suffering. In this foster home his behavior was disruptive and included minor acts of theft

[5]

and vandalism, but the foster parents realized that Billy was expressing his frustrations in an effort to gain attention. After two years he was beginning to settle down with this understanding and caring family when the foster father was transferred to a job in another state. Local foster care rules prevented his going with the family, and Billy moved again.

In the fifth foster home Billy was again placed with experienced foster parents who also recognized his psychological problems. They tried to help him, but he no longer trusted anyone. Billy was not old enough to drive, but he was determined to do so. He felt powerful behind the wheel of a car, and he "borrowed" one from a neighbor. After smashing into another car, Billy found himself in an institution for juvenile offenders. His foster parents were greatly concerned, but they had little hope for a good future for Billy.

Ruth, on the other hand, is an example of a survivor. Some children seem to thrive, even in the environments in which it would seem impossible to do so. In spite of Ruth's separation from her biological family at an early age and her experiences in a series of foster homes, she has been able to secure a good education and become a parent in a stable and comfortable family. Ruth, who was once labeled retarded, is a teacher working toward an advanced degree. Ruth may have found loving care in some of her foster homes that helped her to develop her full potential. Many children do. But too often everyone's child is no one's child.

TRAPPED IN THE FOSTER CARE SYSTEM

Foster care is supposed to be a way-station on the road to being reunited with parents or to being adopted. In reality, foster care may be a long road with many detours and a closed gate at the end. While it is intended to be temporary care, it is often the only kind of care children know for most of their lives. Almost all experts agree that if children spend more than a year and a half in foster care they will probably live out the rest of their childhood in it.

Too many boys and girls become trapped in situations in which they have little hope of returning home or being freed for adoption. For many children the only contact with their biological parents is perhaps a Christmas card, yet this small gesture makes it legally impossible for them to be put up for adoption. Others will not find permanent homes because they have been lost in the system. Social workers say they have "slipped through the cracks."

A sad truth of the foster care system is that all too often children go into care in the first place when other measures might help to stabilize the family and improve its circumstances. An extreme example of unnecessary placement in foster care is cited in the Children's Defense Fund's 1979 report, *Children without Homes*. Mrs. R. and her three pre-school children lived in a rented house and received federal welfare assistance. When her furnace broke, there was no welfare money available to repair it. The house was very cold, and when one of the children developed a severe respiratory infection, Mrs. R. was charged with neglect. Her children were placed in a foster home.

Since the children no longer lived with her, Mrs. R. did not get the same assistance from welfare. The state program for which she qualified did not provide enough money for her to find a place to live, so she moved to the home of her parents in another state. It was then virtually impossible for her to visit her children in their foster home. This situation was not only intolerable from the point of view of the family, it was also unnecessarily expensive for the state. The cost of repairing Mrs. R.'s furnace and allowing the children to return home can hardly compare with the cost to the state of indefinitely maintaining three children in a foster home. Homemakers and other supportive services provided by the state can help make it possible for children to live at home. But many states are, apparently, willing to pay more to keep a child in a foster home or in an institution than to make arrangements for the child to stay home.

Another chronic problem for the foster care system is the shortage of social workers in the area of child care. Social

[7]

workers are supposed to help the children, their natural parents, and the foster parents, but they are often burdened with so many cases that they are unable to give each case the individual attention it requires. As a result, many children suffer from a lack of help from the agencies. With so many children to supervise, so much paperwork, and so many administrative duties, the caseworker spends very little time, on the average, in direct contact with a child each month. A caseworker is most often responsible for seventy-five to ninety children, while the ideal number is only twenty to thirty. How can a social worker understand the individual problems of a foster child in forty-eight minutes a month, the average time for the monthly visits?

Heavy responsibilities, long hours, and low salaries lead to a large turnover of people working in this field. Foster parents sometimes joke among themselves that they are training a new social worker. It is not unusual for a child to be in foster care much longer than the assigned social worker is on the job. And a new caseworker may, in fact, mean a longer stay in foster care.

The children are not the only ones who are neglected because of the shortage of social workers. In many cases an agency has little contact with the biological parents after a child has been removed from the home. The following report is not uncommon: In more than half of the cases in a recent study, a child who was placed in foster care never had a visit from a social worker in the foster home. At the same time, few services were provided to help stabilize and reunite the family. The service most commonly offered, mental health service, reached only 19 percent of the parents whose children were living in foster homes. Sometimes the problem is a lack of funding to support visits from caseworkers, but again it seems that money is available for the wrong things. The following case is an example of the combined problems of unnecessary placement, heavy caseloads, and poor use of funds.

Eight-year-old Carol was placed in a foster home because her emotionally disturbed mother could not cope with the responsibility of caring for the child. A homemaker could have helped Carol's mother make her home a suitable place to live, but there was no homemaker available. When Carol was put in a residential home for children, she became withdrawn and would not speak to anyone. After a month, she refused to eat. When she had not eaten for a week, county caseworkers and administrators decided that she should be sent to a psychiatric hospital for a month. They hoped that psychiatric care and testing would be helpful.

Shortly after Carol was sent to the hospital, her mother reported that she had regained her health and wanted to take Carol home again. Doctors confirmed this report, but when the mother appeared at the county welfare office she was shocked to learn that her daughter had been moved to a psychiatric hospital. This emotional upset played havoc with the mother's progress.

Professional workers who reviewed this case questioned why there had not been more contact with her mother during the time Carol spent at the children's residential center. They suspected that the caseload of the social worker did not permit it. They asked then, as many continue to ask in other cases, "If there is money to institutionalize and hospitalize a child, why is there no money for prevention and early intervention services?"

Improvements in the foster care system could lower the emotional cost to children and the financial burden on the public. But change will come only if enough people care and take action. The passage of the Adoption Assistance and Child Welfare Act of 1980 was one step toward helping the more than half a million children in foster care. Under this law, if a state is to be eligible for federal funding of child welfare programs, it must make a reasonable effort to prevent children from being unnecessarily removed from their homes. The law also encourages efforts that make it possible for children to return home quickly, and provides incentives for states to make other much-needed changes in their systems.

Although the new laws encourage more and faster action toward reuniting children with their families or placing them permanently, it will take many years and much money to untangle the snarls that have developed over the years in the foster care and adoption systems. Children historically have lacked the legal stature and ability to speak for themselves, and the right of parents to determine their children's fate has seldom been challenged. For these reasons, the lot of many children has been grim indeed. One can best understand the foster care and adoption systems of today by exploring how they came to be.

CHAPTER

2

FOSTER CARE YESTERDAY

The present-day foster care system has evolved through a long, interesting history. One of the earliest records of foster care appears in the Biblical story of Moses. In the second chapter of Exodus, Pharaoh's daughter says to Moses' mother, "Take this child away, and nurse him for me, and I will give thee thy wages." In this case, Moses was first adopted by another family, and then, in turn, he was placed temporarily with his own mother. Like most modern foster parents, Moses' mother knew the time must come when she would have to surrender the child to another family.

CARING FOR CHILDREN
IN THE MIDDLE AGES

Until the end of the Middle Ages, children were not treated as separate individuals. Special arrangements were rarely made for children whose parents could not care for them.

From the fall of the Roman Empire, about 476 A.D., until the late 1300's, life for the poorer segment of the population in Western Europe was centered on the manor. All over Europe peasants served the lords of the manor, working in their fields, tending their animals, and doing menial chores in their households. In this system, the sick, the old, and dependent children of the manor were cared for as part of a common family. There was no need for additional private or public charity to provide for boys and girls who did not have their own homes.

Homeless children who were not cared for at the manor were usually helped by the church. Wealthy people gave money to the church, which used one-third of it to aid poor people in the local community, or parish. An early form of the present foster care system was an arrangement by which the church gave money to widows to care for the children of others along with their own children. Priests from the monasteries who visited the sick and the needy and took them food and clothing might be considered predecessors of today's social workers and visiting nurses.

In addition to the church and the manor system, members of the craft and merchants' guilds provided relief for the needy. They treated children the same as adults, however, and expected them to earn their keep by working long hours. Their patterns of child care did not include any efforts to relieve the terrible conditions under which children were forced to live.

THE END OF FEUDALISM

The terrible plague the Black Death swept through Europe, reaching England in 1348. The Black Death took tens of thousands of lives, and created a severe labor shortage. In addition to the many losses from the plague, people were beginning to leave the farms for the cities, lured by new industries that paid high wages. As industries grew and feudalism declined, both the support of children in the manor system and the money available for poor relief from the church also declined. Government relief had to fill the vacuum, but the governments of the day were not inclined to be generous with their money. They strongly encouraged children to be self-supporting; begging was frowned upon. The "deserving poor" were distinguished from beggars who were able to labor but did not.

In England, the laws of Henry VIII, in 1535, imposed harsh penalties on those who refused to work. Sturdy vagabonds were punished by whipping and by having the upper part of their right ears cut away. If they still did not change their ways, they were executed as felons. Children between the ages of 5 and 14 who were caught begging were put to work on farms or to labor in the cities. And the government had the power to see that they did work.

THE POOR LAWS

Disaster in the form of a severe depression struck England during the reign of Elizabeth I, in the late 1500s, and the attitude toward the poor and toward children without caretakers began to change. People started realizing that there were poor people and healthy children who wanted to work but could not find employment. The laws concerning the poor were changed in 1601 with the introduction of the Elizabethan Poor Laws, which remained in effect for over 300 years.

Under the Elizabethan Poor Laws, the local community was responsible for anyone who had been in residence there for as long as three years. Relatives were given the responsibility of caring for any needy person in their family. But if a young child had no relatives, families could bid for the care of the child—and the financial support that went with it. The child, of course, was placed with the family who made the lowest bid, so that the cost to the community would be kept at a minimum. The quality of the home had nothing to do with the decision.

Once children had passed 8 years of age, they were put to work. A girl might be sent to a family, for whom she would do domestic work until she married or reached 21 years of age. A boy would be placed with a tradesman, who would teach him his trade and provide support and some education until the boy was 24 years of age. The boy was called an apprentice and a contract of this kind between a child and master was known as an indenture. This practice was, in fact, the way most young people, even those with parents, learned a trade at this time.

But when orphans were indentured, or bound out as apprentices, the only concern was that the community be spared any expense for their care. No one ever considered the best interests of the child.

A child who did not, or could not, work for a family, a tradesman, a factory employer, a merchant, or a craftsman was sent to the poorhouse along with the old, the sick, the crippled, and others with special problems. Some of the children in poorhouses came as infants with mothers who were sent there. When their mothers left to go to work, the children were often left behind more or less temporarily.

FOSTER CARE IN COLONIAL AMERICA

The Elizabethan Poor Laws had great influence on the laws governing dependent children and adults in the American colonies. During the colonial period, hundreds of children were sent to America from England and other countries to increase the population in the new colonies, where many workers were needed to develop the land. In America, children without homes were cared for in one of three ways. They were apprenticed to a craftsman to learn a trade, sent to the poorhouses, or sent to live with families as indentured servants. The last approach was an early form of foster family care.

In America, as in Europe, it was common for parents to apprentice their sons to master craftsmen who would provide room and board for the child while he learned the trade or craft and worked at menial tasks for the master. Orphans and other children without families, however, could be forcibly indentured by the government. When they were, it was usually as servants, not as apprentices. They worked without pay and many had little expectation of being prepared to earn a living at the end of the term of indenture.

Sometimes children who were living with their parents would also be indentured. In America, as in England, children who were found begging could be bound out without the consent of their parents. And if it appeared that a child was being neglected, the parents could be given an ultimatum: they must indenture the child or the government would do it. This was not so much to protect the child as to protect the public from having to provide support.

The first child in America to be placed by public authority was Benjamin Eaton. He was indentured to a widow for a period of fourteen years at a time when he was probably 7 years old. Even though he did not change homes as often as a child in modern foster care, he did not have the advantage of possibly being adopted. The emphasis was on the benefits to the widow, not on Benjamin's best interests.

The children who were waiting to be bound out as indentured servants lived in poorhouses, which were also known as alms-houses. Some children lived in these asylums for many years before they were placed with families. Placements were often made through advertisements in newspapers, and efforts were rarely made to see if the children were treated well in their new homes. No social workers checked the conditions of the homes to which the children were sent or investigated the characters of people who would act in place of their parents. In some cases town officials checked to see if indentured children were being exploited, but this concern was not universal. As a result, some children fared well, but others were abused in varying degrees by the people for whom they worked.

THE FIRST ORPHANAGES

During the eighteenth and nineteenth centuries, the number of apprenticeships and domestic situations for children who could not live with their biological parents decreased. Children were no longer as useful in homes, and their lack of strength and endurance made some of them an economic liability in factories. Large numbers of children were placed in institutions with criminals, the chronically ill, the poor, the unwanted and homeless elderly, and the emotionally disturbed. These places were filthy, and disease was common.

In response to outcries from people who were alarmed

about the placement of children in these institutions, special homes for children grew in number about the beginning of the nineteenth century. One typical orphanage expressed its purpose in this way: "To rescue from ignorance, idleness and vice, unprotected and helpless children, and to provide for them that support and instruction which may eventually render them valuable members of the community."

The growth of orphanages reflected an increasing concern for the welfare of homeless children. Yet replacing the degrading and unhealthful poorhouses by special institutions for children was no guarantee of humane treatment. These homes varied greatly in the care they gave the children.

Many orphanages took all homeless children, but some specialized in those with certain problems. For example, the New York Asylum for Idiots at Syracuse was established about 1850 for the care of children who were so deficient in intelligence that they could not be educated at an ordinary school. One wonders if some of the children might have shown normal intelligence if they had been brought up in different environments before they entered this home for "idiots." Some of the boys were reported to have made 439 different words from the letters in the word "congregationalist." One pupil in the home was said to have had the habit of driveling at the mouth and of holding his head down, but he learned to read, write, multiply, and subtract, and developed a special interest in arithmetic. He could go to the city and buy what he was told. He was considered self-supporting under proper supervision.

THE EVOLUTION OF PRESENT-DAY FOSTER CARE

The New York Juvenile Asylum, incorporated in 1851, received disobedient, friendless, and neglected children—both boys and girls—between the ages of 7 and 14. Children were kept for an average of one and a half years, after which they were returned to their families or friends, if they had any. If they had none, they were sent to the Western Agency.

[17]

The Western Agency was an administrative center located near Bloomington, Illinois, in a vast farming region. Groups of twenty or thirty children were sent there at seasons of the year when they could be of most help on the farms. The agency would take the children to railroad stations in the area, where farmers who were interested came to see them when they were put on display. A child could be selected to spend two weeks with a family on a trial basis. If all went well, he or she could be indentured to the family. If the trial period was unsuccessful, the child was offered to another family.

In 1853 the Children's Aid Society was formed in New York City with the purpose of rescuing children from the terrible conditions they met on the city streets. Under the leadership of Charles Loring Brace, a young minister who helped found the society, the organization played a major role in placing individual children with families in rural areas. Brace was responsible for finding homes for thousands of dependent and neglected children in what was then considered "the West." Many of the children went only as far as the prairie states, or even northern New York State.

The Children's Aid Society was the first placement agency that was not related to an institution and one of the first that did not indenture the children it placed. Brace's action has been called the beginning of the controversy between those who favored placing children in group homes or orphanages and those who favored placing them in individual, foster homes. Trends toward each type of care have varied through the years and from one state to another, and the quality of care has varied from institution to institution and from family to family.

The evolution and development of new methods of foster care continues today. Group foster homes, which have come into being in recent years, consist of up to a dozen young people who live with foster parents or paid child care workers. Even more recently, alternative group homes, such as runaway houses and group homes in which the counselors are very young, have appeared in an effort to meet the needs of some young people.

The circumstances that bring children to foster care have changed dramatically since the nineteenth century. Today, only about 3 percent of the children who enter foster care have no living parents. Many are the children of parents who have given them up because of temporary hardships such as physical or emotional illness. Child abuse is a major reason why children are placed in foster homes—often involuntarily. In some cases, a child's own emotional problems or antisocial behavior patterns are the reasons for entering foster care. An alarming number of children in foster care have parents who simply do not want them. These are just some of the gates to foster care, but they are gates that open and close behind children more often than necessary.

CHAPTER

3

MOVING INTO FOSTER CARE

Susan's mother gave her milk and cookies when she came home from school, just as she did every day, but today was different. Susan could tell that something was wrong by the way her mother was acting. The extra care and the tears in her eyes were not usual.

Susan could remember many days when her mother had lost her temper and hit her hard. Sometimes the beatings were so bad that they left bruises, and she often kept a jacket on in school to cover the marks on her arms. Recently, though, her teacher had asked about the swelling on her face. Even though Susan had denied that her mother was responsible for the bruises, the teacher had sent her to the school nurse. The nurse, in turn, had reported the problem to the social service department and they had sent a social worker to Susan's home.

At first, her mother had been very angry about this, but lately, Susan could see, she had been trying not to beat her. Her mother tried hard to stop because she really did not want to hurt the girl, but when she was tired and angry, the old habits continued.

Today Susan's mother explained a new plan to her. She

was to stay away from home while her mother tried to learn better ways of expressing her anger. Susan was to live with another family for a while as a foster child.

Susan did not like the idea of being a foster child. Even though things were bad at home, it was her own home and she did not want to live anywhere else. Susan began to blame herself for misbehaving and causing the trouble. In a way, she felt that she was being punished by the arrangement to send her to a foster home. She left her mother for what was meant to be a better life, but it was a long time before Susan could smile again.

MAKING THE TRANSITION
TO A FOSTER HOME

Susan's experience of moving to a foster home and her feelings about it are typical of those of children who have to leave their own homes. Although it is usually circumstances or the parents' behavior that causes the child to move into foster care, many children blame themselves. Like Susan, they feel they are being punished for bad behavior or for angry thoughts about their parents, even though such thoughts are common to all children from time to time. One little boy decided that he had been placed in foster care because he was not a good eater. Since he was placed directly from the hospital, after he was born, it is easy for others to see that this was not the real reason. Still, it is difficult to change the child's misconception. Whenever possible, telling a child the reason for a separation before it takes place can help to limit the amount of guilt he or she carries.

Ideally, every young child who goes into foster care should be told by a parent at least a week before the move is to take place. Older children should know about two weeks ahead, and teenagers will be able to deal with the situation better if they know what is going to happen at least three weeks before they change homes. Many placements are brought about by emergencies, but even when this is the case, it helps if a parent can talk to the child just before he or she leaves home. Children who are told that foster care is part of a larger plan to make things better are fortunate.

There are other ways, too, of making the transition less difficult. If the child's biological parents or parent, the foster parents, and the social worker involved in the case can work together, the move is much easier. With the cooperation of all concerned, it may be possible for a child to visit the foster home before moving there.

On his first visit to his future home, Dan was taken to meet his foster parents and to see the room he would have in their house. On a second visit, he met the other children who lived there. And on the third visit, Dan had dinner with his foster parents and the rest of the new family. When he moved in, the surroundings were familiar and the people were not totally strange. This helped to ease the initial strain a great deal. Many children who are going into foster care find it comforting to take some of their favorite possessions along with them. Family pictures are popular reminders of home.

The way the parent says goodbye is also important to the child's understanding of the separation. Some mothers go with their children on moving day and help them unpack and put their things away in the new room. Children feel better if their parents at least say a definite goodbye, rather than sneak away. A goodbye helps children to know they are not being abandoned. In most cases, separation from parents is difficult for everyone involved.

HOW CHILDREN REACT
TO FOSTER CARE

Children who enter foster care go through a series of stages in their reactions to being separated from their parents. In the first stage, children feel a sense of disbelief. They ask themselves, "How could this happen? There must be some mistake." During the first few days or weeks, many children suffer from colds, lack of appetite, nightmares, or other problems. This is part of the shock of separation. Some children behave unusually well at first, because they feel strange, but this good behavior, which social workers often call the honeymoon, does not last more than a few weeks. Then the children behave the way they did at home.

The second stage of reactions to separation is protest. Children may do everything they can think of to irritate the foster parent in the hope of getting home again. They lash out with anger at all three "parents": the biological parents who sent them into foster care, the social worker who is seen as responsible for the situation, and the foster parents who keep them in it. Children new to foster care are frequently hostile to other children at school because the separation did not happen to them.

Being angry after moving into foster care is normal. So is being sad. It is helpful for children to know that they are not alone in experiencing these feelings. And if children know that it is a good thing to express their feelings in acceptable ways, they do not spend energy hiding them or acting them out in other, harmful ways.

Stage three is known as despair. When a child gives up fighting, perhaps after several months of staying in the foster home, sadness tends to increase. Many children act younger than their years, tend to mope around the house, and appear to want some kind of comfort which, if it is offered, they may not accept because they are not ready for it.

In the fourth, or last, stage, children adjust to foster care. Although they do not get over the separation, they begin to feel better and become more realistic about the situation. Experts believe that the time involved to reach the adjustment stage is usually about nine months, but even then, there may be many problems.

VISITS FROM PARENTS

Often the children who make the best adjustment to foster care are those who have regular contact with their biological parents. In fact, visiting is considered the single most important thing that a parent can do for a child in foster care.

Suppose you have been living at a foster home for two months. You are still feeling angry with your mother for sending you away to a strange family where you have to go to a new school and make new friends. You felt abandoned when your father left a year ago, and you never see him any more. Now you haven't seen your monther for two months, even though she promised to visit you. You know she has been very sick, but sometimes you wonder if she really cares about you. Perhaps she will abandon you, too.

Saturday is visiting day for the two other children who live with you in the foster home. Each week, their mothers come to visit or take them somewhere. Your mother is supposed to come today. Will she really come? What will you say to her? What will she tell you when you ask if you can go home again? But she does not come this Saturday because she is still in the hospital. Your questions go unanswered, but you continue to hope that she will come soon.

Some parents are not able to visit, perhaps because they are ill or live too far away. But other parents choose not to visit their children in foster care, because visiting may arouse unpleasant feelings. Even parents who love their children very much may find visits difficult because they experience feelings of failure, sadness, frustration, and guilt about not being able to keep their children at home. If the foster home is nicer than their own, they may feel some jealousy because they cannot provide such a home.

Equally, foster children may have mixed feelings themselves at visiting time. It is common for them to feel their loyalties divided between biological parents and foster parents. Many biological parents are afraid to let their own children know that it is a good thing to enjoy a stay in a foster home; therefore, children may feel guilty if they are having a good time. Actually, it is better for everyone if the child is happy in a foster home, but some people are afraid that foster parents will "steal" a child's love from them. This attitude also makes them more ready to believe a child's untrue statements about harsh treatment.

Another tactic many children use is to play one set of parents against the other to get something they want. For example, a child may tell a biological parent, "I get to stay up late here," or "I can watch TV as much as I want in this house." Very often these statements are found to be untrue.

A first visit is especially difficult. Even if a private space is provided in the foster home, the situation is artificial. In the usual course of family life, parents do not often sit down at an appointed time and have a long quiet talk with their children. Yet here they are, the two of them, in a stranger's living room with nothing to do for an hour. To make matters worse, some of the child's feelings about the separation will probably surface. Toys, a book, or a game help to ease the situation, but children often turn their backs on their parents, wander off, or act silly at visiting time.

At later visits, children may beg their parents to take them home. After an unpleasant visit in which a child has talked a parent into promising something he or she cannot do, the parent may decide to skip a visit. Or visits may be skipped for any number of reasons, such as personal conflicts, changing work schedules, illness, or a sudden emergency. Even though a visit may make a child anxious, excited, disruptive, or all three, both before and after it occurs, the disappointment of missed visits can create problems just as severe.

FOSTER PARENTS

When a child has had a stressful visit with the biological parent, or is angry and bitter because the parent has missed still another visiting day, it is the foster parent who must attempt to ease the pain. It is the job of the foster parent to restore a sense of normality to a life torn by emotional conflict. Who are the people who take children into their homes and show concern for their feelings as well as the feelings of their biological parents?

People sometimes think that foster parents take children into their homes just to make some extra money, and occasionally that is true. One couple, for example, sought financial help from a local church because the money they expected when they took a foster child did not arrive at once. They had been unable to budget their own income and admitted that they took the boy only because of the extra money for his support.

For the most part, however, foster parents are mature individuals who love and understand children. They must be able to deal with the erratic behavior of children who are adjusting to situations that are difficult for them, to love children who are theirs only temporarily, and to provide care on funds that are usually inadequate. Although many foster parents are in the low to middle income range, payments made to them by social agencies are usually less than the cost of adequate care for the children.

To cope successfully with the financial and emotional problems of foster parenting requires both strength and sensitivity. Ideally, foster families are carefully screened by social workers who help them prepare for the problems that may occur. Many foster children bear scars from conditions in their own homes and some have the added burden of having been moved from one home to another. At first, foster children hold great hope of returning home, but as time goes on they may lose their self-identity and their ability to trust other people. This can cause serious behavior problems.

In addition to the special problems of children who have been living in foster care, foster parents must cope with the supervision by social workers, visits from biological parents, and a host of other differences that are not present in a normal parenting situation. Good foster parenting has been called super-parenting.

An outstanding foster mother can make a real contribution to a child's adjustment and emotional development, as Kim's experience shows. She entered a foster home at three o'clock in the morning because of an emergency situation. There was no time to prepare her for the separation from her mother and father, and she took a long time to adjust to her new home. Kim's foster mother was very patient, but it was difficult for her to understand why Kim insisted on telling lies. Kim told her classmates about presents that her biological mother had sent her, although there had been none. She described her father as a banker, while the truth was that he could not hold a job because of alcoholism. Kim told her foster mother that her father had stopped drinking and that both her parents were coming to take her to a beautiful new home.

Kim's foster mother learned from the social worker on the case that none of this was true. She then realized that Kim had started to believe in a fantasy family that was real in her mind. Because she then understood the source of Kim's lies, the foster mother was able to help Kim accept the real situation.

In recent years, an increasing number of foster parents have become involved in training programs that help them understand the special problems of the children in foster care. But success stories like Kim's are still exceptions in the system as a whole. Certainly there are good foster homes, where living conditions are decent and where foster parents provide loving attention and support, but many children are harmed by the very system of foster care that has been established to help them.

FOSTER CARE DRIFT AND OTHER PROBLEMS

Some foster parents are willing to care for children until they reach adolescence but will not keep them through this difficult age. So foster children find themselves moved from one place to another. "Adrift in foster care" is a common way of describing such children. And it can happen long before they become adolescents.

All too often, foster parents find that even young children are so unmanageable that they can no longer keep them. As long as children are forced to move from one home to another and then another, the system of foster care will be faced with one of its greatest failings.

An extreme but alarming example of foster care drift was reported by the *Tucson Daily Citizen* a few years ago. Twins who had been moved from one foster home to another from the time they were babies were dropped off at a new home when they were 7 years old. The social worker made a request of the new foster mother: "Try to keep them as long as possible. They usually last only three months."

Worse than drifting in foster care is being lost in the system. Those who experience out-of-state placement are the most easily lost, yet many agencies admit that they have no idea how many children have been sent to faraway places. Why are foster children from the north sent to the south and ones from the south sent to the north? Why would a child from an eastern state be placed in a foster home in the west? Sometimes there are good reasons for sending a child far from home. Special care may be needed, but it may not be available in the state in which the child lives. Consider Jimmy, who at 7 years old was both blind and handicapped by a nervous condition that made him twitch. When his parents could no longer care for him, they asked that he be placed in a foster home. Since no foster parents in the community would accept this child, arrangements were made to send him to a residential facility in a distant state, which cared for children with this kind of handicap. But his parents could not visit him there because of the cost of transportation. They tried to communicate by letters, but even when they wrote to the administrators of the home, no one answered.

Jimmy's case is not unusual. Records of children who are placed out of state make a maze of crossing tracks on a map of the United States. Studies show that some states seem to be exchanging children. Certainly, reports are conflicting. For instance, one state counted 287 children coming from 18 other states at a time when 22 states reported sending children there. And the federal government, which controls interstate movement of goods and agricultural produce, has been accused of keeping better records of the number of chickens that cross state borders each month than the number of children who are placed in other states.

A number of studies of where children move while they are in foster care have made the public aware of some alarming conditions. For example, the Children's Defense Fund and some similar groups that monitor violations of children's rights brought suit against the state of Louisiana on behalf of about 600 children who had been placed in Texas. Poignant testimony by a visitor from Louisiana who was investigating the case showed that the children were aching for contact with home and desperately wanted to return there. They begged the visitor to tell them about their homes in Louisiana and to come to see them again. This visit was unusual, for in general no effort had been made to find out what was happening to the children who were placed out of state. Although Louisiana officials were legally required to visit facilities in their own state, they did not have to go out of state. When the children were examined as a result of the lawsuit, evidence of repeated abuse and neglect was found—in addition to the abuse and neglect involved in not trying to bring the children back to their homes or to less restrictive foster homes in their own communities.

While some efforts have been and are still being made to correct the abuse of children who are placed far from home, out-of-state placement is still a fact of life for many children. Continuing public awareness and concern are needed if the children who move into foster care are to be placed as near their homes as possible. Also needed are better methods of following the lives of those who are sent far away. Just being placed near home, however, does not exempt some children from living in extremely difficult situations. For the child who lives in as many as eighteen different foster homes or the child who lives with roaches, rats, and rotting floors, foster care may be worse than the care they received in their original homes. After months of intensive inquiry, the National Commission on Children in Need of Parents reported in 1979 that, "with some admirable exceptions, the foster care system in America was an unconscionable failure." No wonder there is increasing concern for children who must move into foster care, and an urgent need to find alternatives to the present system.

CHAPTER

4

"WHERE WILL I BE ON MY BIRTHDAY?"

Nick was 5 years old when, one day, a lady and a man came to his home and wanted to talk to him. He had never seen them before, but they said they were his friends. The only friend Nick knew was his puppy, and he didn't understand why these people now wanted to take him for a ride in their car. Nor did Nick understand why his mother was crying when she agreed that he should go with the couple, even though they refused to take his puppy along, too. Nick could not understand why they took him to the police station or why they asked so many questions about how his father treated him. Above all, Nick didn't understand why the lady and the man didn't take him home when he had answered their questions. Instead they took him to a strange house and told him the people there would be his parents for a while. These new people were very nice, but Nick did not understand why they would not take him home.

When Nick's mother came to visit she told him that his puppy had run away. She promised to buy him a new one when he went home again, but Nick still wondered when that would be. A lady from the social agency comes to visit Nick every few months and tells him he will go home after a while, but now he thinks it may be a very long time.

[34]

Nick and thousands of foster children like him live in a world of unanswered questions. Where will I be on my birthday? Where will I be for the holidays? When can I go home? Uncertainty about the future is a painful fact of life. In an attempt to correct this situation, efforts to improve the foster care system have come to focus on providing permanent arrangements for the children of distressed families. These approaches generally fall into three categories: Preventing a child's entering foster care by helping the family through crises; working toward an early return of the child to his or her home; and releasing the child for adoption at an early age.

KEEPING THE FAMILY TOGETHER

One new approach that is helping families stay together—or be reunited quickly—involves the use of "homebuilder therapists." These workers spend as much time as necessary during a six-week period helping families resolve crises and learn new ways of managing problems. For example, when service agencies in Tacoma, Washington, launched a homebuilders program, they found that the need for placing children out of their homes was reduced by 87 percent over a period of three years. Follow-up studies showed that the positive results of the intervention continued well after the six-week period.

In one case, a homebuilder worked with a family that seemed to have a crisis every week and had received help—or attempts at help—from practically every social agency in town. The 16-year-old girl was in foster care after being badly beaten by the father, but three other children were still living at home. The mother was emotionally ill, and the father asserted himself by making threats and beating the children. Most of the people who knew the family thought it was probably hopeless to expect them to remain together.

On the first visit, the homebuilder sat at the kitchen table with the family and talked with them about their problems as best she could. The father was under great stress. He felt that everything was falling apart because the eldest girl had left and the 12- and 14-year-old girls wanted to leave home. According to him, everything had blown up and he couldn't take it anymore. The mother giggled hysterically and contributed nothing of value to the conversation. The 12 year old sat silently hunched in her chair and the 14 year old chain-smoked. The 3 year old had a voice that sounded like a man's. The older girls explained that this was the result of nodules on her vocal chords that came from excess crying. Everyone ignored her when she crawled on the drainboard and took food out of the cupboard. They even ignored her when she came to the table and hit people.

Since the social worker was afraid that the father would lose his temper and hurt the girls if she left them at that point, she called three other therapists to join her that evening. They talked to the parents and the older girls on a one-to-one basis, and before they left they felt that the situation was under control for that night.

By the end of six weeks, the father had been helped to recognize his irritation while it was still at a low level and respond to his anger before it overwhelmed him. The mother, who had been virtually a prisoner at home for sixteen years, was helped to work toward goals that eventually enabled her to become a beautician. The children were helped with their problems, and their behavior improved.

To accomplish these results, the family was given over a hundred hours of counseling in a six-week period, but a year later the family situation was good. Whether or not this homebuilder approach, and others that prevent foster care, are financially better for taxpayers is hard to determine, but it is known that the cost of one child in long-term foster care is about $20,000 to $60,000 for a period of a few years, many times over the cost of home care. The emotional benefits to the family and generations to come cannot be measured.

Changes in attitudes among child welfare professionals are also helping to keep children in their own homes and out of foster care. The child welfare system once operated on the belief in a "rescue fantasy"—that it was right and proper "to take poor little children out of the terrible homes and put them

[36]

in nice clean places." Today the system is taking a new look at itself and developing new standards. This change in attitude has occurred partly because social workers have become more sensitive to the ways in which people of various cultures cope with their problems.

An especially significant example of cultural differences in solving family problems is seen in some American Indian tribes. The number of American Indian children placed in foster care and adoptive homes is grossly out of proportion to their percentage of the population. This situation may change with better understanding and appreciation of cultural differences. At present, efforts are being made to return greater responsibility and authority for Indian child welfare to the tribes, some of which prohibit removal of their children for foster care or adoption.

PATHWAYS OUT OF FOSTER CARE

Foster care is, of its very nature, supposed to be temporary—to provide care for children during periods when their own families cannot fulfill that responsibility. Ideally, the foster child will be able to return home quickly, and indeed, social workers and legal agencies feel a heavy sense of duty to return children to their biological parents. All too often, however, this goal is clearly impossible to achieve because parents have incurable problems or simply do not want their children. It then becomes essential to find a permanent home for the child before the "temporary" situation of foster care becomes the established pattern of life. One of the most important goals of foster care today is the release of children when they are young if it seems likely that the parents will never be able to care for them adequately. Aggressive planning and improved casework techniques help to free many children for adoption.

A project called Freeing Children for Permanent Placement is an outstanding study in overcoming barriers to planning for the future of children in foster care. This study was funded by the federal government and carried out by the children's division of the Oregon Department of Human Resources. The Oregon Project, as the study is known, enlisted a staff of eleven caseworkers, each of whom was given a small number of families with whom to work. The caseworkers developed close contacts with the biological parents of children who had been in foster care for at least a year and who were considered unlikely to return home. The program succeeded in its purpose by showing that intervention by caseworkers can play a dramatic role in shortening the length of stay in foster care. By the end of the first three years, 26 percent of the children in the project had returned to their biological parents, and 36 percent were living in adoptive homes after parental rights had been terminated.

As a result of the Oregon Project and other studies, many states have been able to find previously unknown pathways for children out of foster care. For example, subsidized adoption, which was once in limited use, is now widely available. Adoption by foster parents was once frowned on or even not permitted, but today it is a popular approach to permanent planning for the child. And attitudes about releasing children whose parents cannot be located have also become more liberal.

In all of these approaches, more frequent and more thorough review of cases leads to faster action to place children permanently. A review of the situation may even bring to light conditions that result in restoring a child to the biological parents. One such case is cited in the report of the Oregon Project. Chris was a happy 9-year-old boy who was living in a stable foster home. He had been placed in foster care at the age of 2 because his father had abused him. The father, who was serving a prison term, appeared to be seriously disturbed, and the likelihood of his ever being able to care for the child seemed remote. Chris's mother was a Japanese woman who had divorced his father and remarried. She appeared to be living happily with her new husband and their 3-year-old son.

Even though Chris's mother had contacted him only about three times each year, she was not uninterested. At the time that he had been placed in foster care, his mother had had a limited grasp of the English language, and cultural differences had prevented her from questioning the outcome of the father's trial. When the case was reviewed, 9-year-old Chris still showed strong emotional ties to his own mother, even though the foster parents were providing good care. Arrangements were made for Chris to return to his own mother. In the months that followed, he became more relaxed and his school work improved. Now his family included his own mother, a stepfather and half-brother, *and* the foster parents, who filled the role of aunt and uncle. This is only one of the cases in which a careful review of the situation enabled a child to return home.

Margaret's case resulted in a different exit from foster care. When she was 18 months old, her mother suffered a psychotic episode in which she stabbed the child and held her under a hot shower in an effort to "spare the child from the degradation of the devil." Margaret was severely burned.

Margaret's mother underwent psychiatric treatment for a year, and then began visiting her in the foster home where she had been placed. Whenever the child caught sight of her mother, she cried and clung to her foster mother. She began having nightmares that caused her to wake up screaming at least once every night. A psychiatrist who studied both the mother and the child found that the child had been so upset by her early experience that she would never be able to accept her mother. Parental rights were terminated when Margaret was 5 years old, and she was adopted by her foster parents. The night she was told of the adoption, the nightmares ceased.

TERMINATING PARENTAL RIGHTS: A CONTROVERSIAL ISSUE

Cases of terminating parental rights are not always so clear-cut. They often raise some thorny questions, and the legal, social, and psychological implications can be far-reaching.

The true story of the "Jones" family is a case in point. Only the names have been changed here. When Darlene Smith was 15 years old, she met 25-year-old Chuck Jones. Darlene hated school, and she hoped to get pregnant so she could be married, settle down, and raise a family. That is just what she did. Her first child, George, was born in April of 1959, and by the time he was 6 years old, he had a sister and three brothers. He already showed many behavior problems. Neighbors reported that George pulled up their flowers, cursed at them, beat up the small children in the neighborhood, and threw rocks at people and cars.

The Jones family suffered from many problems—lack of education, lack of money, and lack of the ability to cope with everyday situations. Neighbors who complained about George's destructive behavior were responsible for his being placed in foster care from age 6 to age 9. But his years in foster care had not improved his behavior. When George returned home, the neighbors continued to complain about his rock throwing and other aggressive behavior.

In the same year that George returned home, neighbors were called to his home by the frightened children and were shocked to find that his mother had given birth, unattended, to her sixth child.

Continued complaints from neighbors about the Jones family brought a social worker to the house. She found only a package of frozen peas in the refrigerator. Dirty dishes sat in scummy sink water and conditions seemed as deplorable as the neighbors had said they were. Her decision to place the children in foster care took just twenty minutes. Soon officers of the juvenile court appeared at the house with a petition enabling them to take away the six children because their parents could neither control them nor adequately care for them.

Rounding up the children for a ride to the juvenile center was not easy. Two boys ran away, the mother pleaded for her lawyer, and the grandmother screamed to prevent the officers from taking the baby. In spite of this, it was not long before the six Jones children, aged 6 months to 10 years, were placed in a temporary home for delinquent and neglected children. This was their gateway to the bureaucratic labyrinth of foster care.

During the next seven years, the Jones children were victims of a tug-of-war between parents who were officially judged to be unfit to care for them and a child welfare system that did not help them either. The four younger boys were shuffled through twenty-three foster homes and institutions during a period of six years. The legal judgment that their parents were unfit meant they could not go home; yet they could not be adopted because their parents would not give consent.

Much of the argument centered on the controversial issue of whether or not the state has the right to break up a family because the parents fail to meet arbitrary standards of competence, morality, or conduct. Some people saw the government as a heartless agent wrenching children from parents because the parents were poor and slow to learn. Others saw the government as a caring agency that saved the children from horrible conditions. One social worker insisted that the parents were not fit to have the children, but another one argued that even incompetent parents are better than no parents.

After a number of court hearings, the right of the Joneses to raise their five sons was legally terminated, although the slightly retarded daughter was allowed to remain with the parents. The primary objective of the termination was to make the boys available for adoption, but the parents immediately appealed the ruling, and the children were trapped in a legal limbo. They could not be released for adoption until the appeal was considered by a higher court.

One of the workers who was concerned with the case admitted that the children were "hung on the wall," their futures suspended. He defended this situation by asking what would have happened if he had just gone along with the judge's decision, placed them for adoption, and then found the termination order overturned by the supreme court of the state. Disagreements about what should and should not have been done fill the case record. Through it all, the children were plagued with emotional and behavioral problems.

The long legal battle over whether the Jones children should be separated from their parents ended about six and a half years after it began. At that time, a federal judge ruled that the termination of the parents' rights was unconstitutional; the children should return to their home.

At this time, social workers noted that in spite of some efforts to improve the home situation, it was not much different from the time the children had left it. The backyard was littered with debris, old tires, and a gutted mattress. Inside, a platter of fried fish left over from the night before sat on a long table that was covered with empty soda cans. The two tiny bedrooms were cluttered, and piles of dirt had been swept together here and there on the linoleum floor. Worn-out chairs and a television set almost completely filled the living room.

While the parents hoped for a happy ending to their problems, a caseworker concluded that there would be many endings as each child grew up and tried to raise a family. With such a history of instability in their own family, it will be hard for these children to become successful parents in their turn. Not everyone agrees that reuniting this family served the best interests of the children.

Should the Jones family have been separated in the first place? What would have happened if they had received help in their home? What would have happened if the children had been freed for adoption when they were young? No one can answer these questions. It is known that the wisdom of removing these children from their parents in the first place was questioned a number of times during the years the children remained in limbo.

The Jones case is not unique, although the outcome can vary from one family to another. Nevertheless, the termination of parental rights almost always involves a long and painstaking procedure. Those who refuse to relinquish their rights voluntarily face far more than a court scene with a solemn black-robed judge determining the future of a young child while parents and the state clash in high drama. Before the case comes to court, a social worker must document all casework activity to build evidence for a court hearing. All possible services must have been offered to the family and it must be shown that the parents repeatedly and conclusively failed to respond.

A family known as the Hoovers was presented by the Oregon Project as a typical case in which the parents' conduct was such that adoption was the goal of permanent placement.

At the time the Hoover children were taken into custody, the parents were 22 and 23 years old. The four children were ages 5, 3, 2, and 2 months. The health department had had many complaints from neighbors, who reported that the children were neglected. One caller reported that the children had been left in the care of an 11-year-old cousin while the parents visited a tavern. And investigations showed that the children were dirty, inadequately clothed, and had skin rashes and burns. The house was described as not fit to live in.

It took five years from the time the Hoover children first entered foster care until the time when they were placed in adoptive homes. During this time extensive efforts were made to rehabilitate the parents so that they would be able to provide adequate care for their children, but a combination of problems, including alcohol abuse, prevented any real progress. The parents were eventually divorced. By the time of the hearing on the petition to terminate the mother's parental rights, the children had been in foster care so long and had seen so little of her that they did not really consider her their mother. Mrs. Hoover's fantasies included hope for a job, a home, financial support from her ex-husband, and an end to drunkenness. However, she could not bring herself to take the actual steps necessary to make any of these hopes a reality.

The father's parental rights were terminated because he had not made the changes necessary to permit the return of his children. He rarely kept visiting appointments, was unable to find a job and pay child support, and made little effort to care for their physical and emotional needs.

It was considered in the best interests of the children that they be adopted and have parents on whom they could depend for loving care and physical necessities. The three older boys were adopted by their foster parents. The youngest child lived with a different set of foster parents, who were unable to keep him because of their advanced age. He was adopted by new parents, with the understanding that his former foster parents could visit in the role of foster grandparents.

Not all cases of permanent placement take as long as the Hoovers'. In cases of desertion, abandonment, or parents' voluntarily relinquishing rights, adoption can often be accomplished in less than a year.

For years, many children were forced to remain in foster care indefinitely because the whole matter of a parent's rights was considered untouchable. Certainly, determining whether or not parental rights should be terminated is difficult and often controversial, but there is increased recognition today that parenthood does not automatically confer the desire to care for children or the skills necessary for doing so.

Balanced against the parent's right to have custody of a child is the right of the child not to be neglected and the responsibility of the state to protect the neglected or abused child. Many decisions today are being made "in the best interest of the child," but some experts warn against ending rights of parents too easily. There is particular concern about penalizing parents for poverty or illness. It may often be wise to terminate parental rights automatically if a parent is unable to provide satisfactory care after a six-month probationary period, but consider the following situation. A mother who is suffering from depression tries a number of drugs prescribed by her doctor. After a year, the right combination of drugs helps her to overcome her problems and she tries to retrieve her child from foster care. An adoption that took place after six months of foster care would mean the mother could not have her child. It is easy to see why termination of parental rights is a complex problem.

CITIZEN ADVOCACY
OF CHILDREN'S RIGHTS

Regardless of the complexities of the problems surrounding the adoption of children in foster care, this issue must be confronted, if children are to avoid endless drifting in foster care. Throughout the United States there is a growing awareness of the issue, and it is being addressed at several levels.

The federal government, which became involved in foster care through the Aid to Families with Dependent Children program in the Social Security system, has encouraged permanent placement by the Adoption Assistance and Child Welfare Act of 1980. This law sets specific goals of permanent placement by requiring a description of the steps taken by the state to achieve it for any child remaining in foster care more than twenty-four months. The status of each child must be reviewed periodically no less frequently than once every six months in order to determine whether or not foster care should continue and whether or not the placement is appropriate. A plan for each child should include, among other things, the projection of a likely date by which the child may be returned home or placed for adoption or legal guardianship, a form of permanent care with relatives, friends, or foster parents. These goals were stated in 1980, to be effective in October 1983.

The passage of legislation does not always assure that its intent will be fully carried out. Political changes in Washington and at the state level can bring in new administrations with different philosophies that affect the enforcement of the laws. Budget cuts may take money away from a program, and enthusiasm for its implementation may wane when its advocates are out of office. Citizens must be aware of the provisions of new laws and check to make certain that they are carried out. Today many people who are concerned about children are joining together in child advocacy groups to speak for children who are too young to influence lawmakers and others with power over their destinies. One of the chief functions of these advocacy groups is to protect those who cannot live with their own families. For example, the Institute for Child Advocacy in Ohio exists because some citizens of that state believe what *should* be happening to children is not always happening. This group was formed to create a voice on behalf of Ohio's children and to see that they are provided with the kind of care they should have. One of its many activities is bringing to the public's attention the difference between the rights and protection to which children are entitled by law or public policy and the actual implementation and enforcement of such rights and protection.

Children's advocates have also found that periodic reviews of foster care cases are a good beginning to a better life for many children. A number of states have established new systems in which family courts must periodically reexamine in detail the situation of children in care. In South Carolina, a citizen review approach has shown outstanding results. With citizens acting as advocates, over 30 percent of a group of children were moved out of foster care within the first six months, and an unusually large number of children were freed for adoption.

In many states, however, review systems have not been so successful, and everywhere there is still much work to be done. The awareness of deficiencies in the foster care system must lead to action for change so that fewer children will need to ask, "Where will I be on my birthday?"

CHAPTER

5

PARENTS IN SEARCH OF CHILDREN

Foster parents may always be in short supply, but the number of people who want to become adoptive parents is huge. These people search for children in many ways and in many places.

Traditionally, couples have adopted babies from agencies that specialize in finding homes for infants whose mothers choose to give them up at birth. Today, however, relatively few young women follow the course of action recently taken by Sally.

Sally considered her options when she discovered that she was pregnant. She did not want to marry the baby's father, because she felt that she could never grow to love him. She did not believe in abortion, and she thought long and hard about the possibility of trying to raise the child herself. It would be difficult, though, without considerable financial help. Even if she could find enough money, Sally was young and ready for a career in the business world. She did not want to be tied down to the responsibilities of caring for a baby. In the end she chose to give up her baby for adoption. Sally's choice was not a popular one; it is estimated that as many as 93 percent of the children who are born to unmarried mothers are *not* offered for adoption at birth.

Throughout most of human history adoption services were designed to benefit parents—both biological and adoptive. People wanted an heir to continue a family name and inherit property, or they wanted a baby to fill emotional needs. During the first half of the twentieth century, the fitness of the baby and its similarity to the adoptive parents were the main concerns. At the same time, unmarried girls wanted to hide their pregnancies from the world to avoid the shame connected with bearing a child that society called illegitimate. This meant that many babies came into the world in need of homes. Adoption agencies could take great pains to match the physical characteristics and natural abilities of biological and adoptive parents.

With the increased use of birth control and the availability of abortion to prevent the birth of unwanted babies, the number of available infants has decreased tremendously. Society, too, has become generally more accepting of single mothers, regardless of their marital status, and improvements in child care facilities now free single women to work to support their children financially. These developments have brought radical changes to the adoption process for both parents in search of children and children who need parents. Many homes for expectant mothers that once had large adoption programs now concentrate on helping young mothers care for their children. Some teach parenting skills to abusive parents with children of all ages. While many agencies are concerned about the unrealistic plans of some girls who want to keep their babies, they are reluctant to emphasize the advantages of adoption. On rare occasions an agency has been accused of pressuring a girl to place her baby with adoptive parents through the agency and has been involved in a legal suit when the biological mother changed her mind.

ADOPTING A BABY OVERSEAS

For adoptive parents who insist on a baby, the waiting period is usually long and the path is often difficult. Many choose to adopt foreign children. Betsy and Jack, for example, are 30 years old and want a baby very much. They have been trying unsuccessfully to adopt a baby in the United States for three years. Today, finally, they are on a plane to South America, where they hope to begin adoption proceedings for the little girl whose picture they have been looking at many times each day.

Their adoption procedure, however, is an expensive and complicated one. With the help of a local agency recommended by the Foreign Adoption Center, Betsy obtained an application from an orphanage in Colombia, South America. After she and her husband had filled out the forms, they returned them to the orphanage with copies of their marriage license and birth certificates. Several months passed, during which the local agency made a home study to evaluate the parents. Finally a letter arrived offering Betsy and Jack a 2-week-old baby who had to be picked up at the orphanage in Colombia within six weeks. The agency then sent a copy of the home study to the orphanage, and soon after that the baby's birth certificate and adoption release arrived in the mail. Betsy and Jack had been accepted as adoptive parents for the baby.

During the next few weeks, the couple arranged for two airline tickets to Colombia. They made sure their passports were in order, obtained a Colombian tourist card, and made other arrangements for their trip. Betsy and Jack are carrying a certified check for $5,000 for the Colombian lawyer who has made the necessary arrangements in that country. In a few hours now they hope to hold their new daughter in their arms. Their excitement is almost beyond control.

Betsy and Jack will spend about ten days in Colombia completing legal arrangements and getting a U.S. visa, for which prearranged approval has been granted by the Immigration and Naturalization Service in their hometown. Since foreign children who are adopted by American citizens do not have to wait to enter the United States under the quota system, visas for their entrance to the United States are easily approved. A local doctor will check the health of the baby, and Betsy, Jack, and their daughter will return home together.

The legal work, however, will continue for several years.

After their lawyer files the adoption petition in the state in which they live, Betsy and Jack will be supervised by a court-appointed representative or a local adoption agency. Two years after the legal adoption in the United States, the child will be eligible for United States citizenship.

Whether the adoptive parents go to a foreign country for their child, or whether the child flies to the United States with an escort, most international adoptions appear to be accomplished successfully if there is guidance from a reputable international adoption program. Some of the agencies that help people who are interested in foreign adoptions are listed on pages 80 to 81.

However, this method of adoption is not without its drawbacks and frustrations. There are stories of people who pay adoption fees and arrive in distant lands only to find there is no child waiting for them. And even abandoned babies in other countries are not always readily available for adoption. In some countries adoption is seen as a form of imperialism, and other countries consider adoption as unwanted charity, or have customs that prevent it.

BLACK MARKET ADOPTIONS

The shortage in the United States of white babies without handicaps has led to some questionable and even highly unscrupulous adoption practices. Some of these adoptions are outright illegal, because large amounts of money change hands. This is the black market, in which babies are in effect bought and sold. In the so-called "gray market," no large amount of money is involved. Perhaps a doctor who has a pregnant patient willing to give up her child for adoption also has friends who desperately want such a baby. The doctor may or may not consider the qualifications of his friends in the light of what is best for a baby. Nevertheless, private adoptions of this type are legal in most states.

Sometimes medical fees, legal fees and travel expenses are paid by the adoptive parents, but the main concern is bringing together would-be parents and a child. Many people who are involved in gray market adoptions justify their actions by claiming that agency standards are arbitrary, prejudiced, or overly stringent. In adoption agencies, these people feel, the determination of the suitability of both parents and children is left to the personal judgment of social workers who may or may not be wise in their decisions. Very often agencies are understaffed and workers are underpaid; these conditions slow procedures to what seems an impossible time period for those who are searching for a child.

If gray market adoptions are widespread, illegal adoptions of "black market" babies are believed to be a booming racket. Here the only qualifications the parents need are the ability to pay a large sum of money and the willingness to be involved in an arrangement that involves laundered money, false court documents, and cash payoffs. There are no safeguards for these adoptive parents. There is no receipt for money paid and no way of checking information provided. While some efforts have been made to prevent unscrupulous people from trafficking in infants, it is difficult to enforce laws that prohibit such transactions.

Black market babies have always been more or less available to parents in search of a child. Even in the days when there were more babies available for adoption, there were couples who could not pass the screening of adoption agencies and who had no connections with obstetricians willing to help in a placement. These people contacted "baby brokers" who enlisted the support of clinics and hospitals to help them find girls who might be willing to have their babies and give them up for a fee. People involved in the schemes made large sums of money from couples who were too old, who did not meet conventional moral standards, or who did not want to wait until an agency baby was available.

A black market arrangement might follow this pattern: Mr. and Mrs. Baker have decided that they are ready to have a baby, but Mrs. Baker does not conceive as planned. They visit a doctor, who examines both of them and discover that Mrs. Baker has a medical problem that will prevent her from ever

[52]

becoming pregnant. Since they always plan ahead, they have already moved into a larger house and picked out the room that will be the nursery. After the doctor suggests that they adopt a child, Mrs. Baker calls the local agency. To her sorrow, Mrs. Baker finds that the agency is no longer taking names for its list of parents who are waiting for a baby. Their suggestion that she consider an older child does not appeal to her at all. The Bakers want a baby to take the place of the one they planned to have.

Mr. and Mrs. Baker are very depressed, but when, a friend tells them about someone who found a baby through an attorney in another state, they can barely wait to contact him. Mr. Michael, the attorney, assures them that he can help. He has a package arrangement by which they will be certain of getting a baby for a fee of over $10,000. They can even have some choice in the matter.

Mr. Michael explains that he has many contacts in southern states, where there are large numbers of girls whose babies need homes. Theirs would be a wonderful home for one of these poor children. Actually, Mr. Michael is part of what is sometimes called a baby mill. He works with a colleague who contacts pregnant girls and persuades them to give up their babies for a fee. The girls are housed in a pleasant place where they can swim, be tutored, enjoy each other's company, and await the birth of the babies who will bring them much-wanted money.

Mr. and Mrs. Baker are sent several case studies with information about the background of the girls and the probable fathers of the babies they expect. The Bakers choose to take the baby of a girl who is expecting it in December, but this baby is born prematurely and dies two days after birth. Mr. Michael tells the Bakers not to worry. Their arrangement assures them of a baby, and he will see that they are next on the list.

When "their" baby is born, the Bakers will fly to Mexico and meet Mr. Michael. He will bring the child to a hotel in a small border town in order to evade the U.S. authorities. The adoption is handled quickly and discreetly, and the proud new parents fly home with their son. They may, of course, be good parents for him. On the other hand, because they wanted a child so very badly, they may be indulgent, overprotective parents who do not help him become a responsible member of society as he grows up.

Because the people engineering black market adoptions are motivated solely by money, no one will be thinking of how the adoptive home will serve the interests of the child. But as long as people are willing to pay a price for a baby, there will be those who are eager to make the arrangements.

CONTROVERSIAL ADOPTIONS

A relatively new adoption practice, and a highly controversial one, is the use of the surrogate mother. When a husband is not fertile, his wife can often be made pregnant through artificial insemination, but when a woman cannot have a child, the problem is more complicated. Some women who enjoy being pregnant have agreed to bear children for women who cannot do it themselves. These women are called surrogate mothers. Usually, the sperm from the infertile woman's husband is artificially placed in the surrogate mother. As soon as the child is born, the biological father files a petition in court asking for custody of the baby. His wife files another petition to adopt the child legally.

Surrogate mothering is not new. The Book of Genesis says that when Abraham's wife, Sarah, could not conceive, arrangements were made for her maid Hagar to have a child by Abraham. Hagar was called a concubine rather than a surrogate mother, and the child was fathered by natural intercourse rather than artificial insemination, but the arrangement was similar in other ways.

Today there are many women who are willing to bear the child badly wanted by a friend or relative and to give up that child for adoption. One single woman expressed the desire to experience pregnancy and to do something worthwhile for society. This woman gave birth to a baby girl who was adopted by the biological father and his wife. Even after several years, the surrogate mother remained in contact with the girl's parents.

The controversy arises when the surrogate mother is paid a fee. Every state prohibits the buying and selling of children, and so legal questions are raised if a woman receives money for having another's baby.

The Surrogate Parenting Association of Louisville, Kentucky, began matching surrogate mothers with couples who want children by this method in August of 1979. This organization claims to have many surrogate mothers in the process of bearing children. One of these mothers, however, made public the fact that as a surrogate, she had given birth to a baby for the payment of a fee. This led to a controversy in Kentucky, where the baby was born and surrendered to the parents who were involved in the contract. Court decisions in Kentucky and in Michigan have called surrogate mothering for a fee illegal, but the decisions have been appealed. Questions other than legal ones have been raised in connection with surrogate parenting. What would happen if the child were defective and the adoptive parents decided not to accept it? What if a surrogate mother felt that she could not part with the child to whom she had given birth? These and other questions are being considered even in cases where the only exchange of money is that needed for medical bills, and studies are under way in several states to determine the need for legislation about this kind of childbearing and adoption.

An equally controversial issue in the area of adoption is the relationship of children, their biological parents, and their adoptive parents. This is often called the adoption triangle. For many years adoption records were tightly sealed with the idea of protecting both sets of parents. Biological parents had no fear of future recriminations because of their actions, and adoptive parents were protected from being harassed by those who might change their minds after legally relinquishing their children. Today, an experimental approach to adoption gives both adoptive and biological parents the option of exchanging names and arranging visits. The adoptive parents have a chance to discuss personal histories and beliefs and the biological parent or parents are given a chance to feel more comfortable about giving up their children for adoption. This procedure, which has always been considered unthinkable by most agencies, is being sponsored by the Pierce-Warwick Adoption Service in Washington, D.C., and the Adoption Research Council also in Washington, D.C.

Linda Cannon Burgess, a social worker who has been involved with adoptions for over twenty years, would take this approach even farther, advocating adoptions in which the two sets of parents communicate during a child's growing years. While open adoption has been practiced among some families of blacks, Eskimos, Hawaiians, and others for many generations, it has been done informally and without a stigma of illegitimacy. Ms. Burgess thinks the time has come for the practice to become more widespread throughout America. She believes open adoption could relieve the fantasies of many adopted adolescents, who imagine that their real parents were superior people and would never treat them the way their adoptive parents do. And, most important, she feels it would encourage more women to give up their babies for adoption rather than have abortions or try to raise them by themselves.

Certainly until more mothers do want to place their healthy, white infants with adoptive parents, people who insist on the perfect, "gold-plated baby" will continue their often-frustrating search. But this is only one side of the adoption picture. In the next chapter we shall look at the children who are waiting for adoptive homes.

CHAPTER

6

CHILDREN WHO WAIT

If there are 25,000 children in the United States who are free for adoption, and many more who could be free, why must parents search so hard to find children? It is because many people will accept only a white infant with no handicaps. Bob and Kirsten Smith, however, are taking a different path. They are adopting a special child, one who was hard to place because of his age and physical handicap. Their new son, Tommy, has spent five years in foster homes, but this time his suitcase will be unpacked for a permanent stay. The Smiths will take him to specialists to see if something can be done to improve his twisted leg so that he can run and play, but if the condition cannot be changed, they will love him just the same.

At 5 years old, Tommy is beyond the age many parents would accept for adoption. Yet most of the children who are released for adoption fall into the 4-to-14-year age group, with as many as 40 percent over the age of 11. Many of these children develop emotional problems if they are moved from one foster home to another, and Bob and Kirsten expect some difficult behavior from a boy who has lived in many different places. But they are willing to look for his strengths and take the bad with the good.

Tommy and his adoptive family represent a growing trend in adoption practices. With such a scarcity of "gold-plated babies," many agencies have refused to accept as clients parents who are unwilling to accept older children, biracial children, or children with handicaps. Today many agencies consider no child unadoptable, for even the most difficult to place are being adopted into families at an increasing rate. This change has resulted in part from financial assistance provided by the government to families that adopt children with handicaps. It is also a result of efforts to publicize these children's needs.

REACHING PARENTS
THROUGH TELEVISION

You might hear about a child who needs a home through a television program such as *Wednesday's Child* in Oklahoma. This program grew out of a discussion some newsmen had about community problems that viewers might help to solve. Early in 1979, KOCO–TV's news anchorman, Jack Bowen, decided to raise public awareness by introducing hard to place children in a sensitive way. Each week a television cameraman followed Mr. Bowen on an outing to the zoo or other interesting place with a child who was available for adoption. The film was shown on the program *Wednesday's Child,* with information about the child for prospective parents. The response was outstanding. During a fourteen-month period, forty-seven children appeared on the air and thirty-two of them were adopted. Most of the other fifteen were in the process of being adopted by the end of that period. In addition, there were forty-five related adoptions—cases in which viewers responded to a child on *Wednesday's Child,* but adopted another hard to place child who had not been shown on television.

In the beginning, social agencies were resistant to the idea of the program, but they soon recognized its many positive results. After the program began, some foster children asked their social workers if they could appear on it, a fact that indicates that they did not feel the children were being exploited in any way. Many foster children who had hidden the fact that they lived away from their biological parents even became comfortable about revealing that they lived in foster homes. Always, though, the children who participated were consulted and required to give their consent to having their stories broadcast.

Similar programs, such as Philadelphia's *Friday's Child,* provide exposure for some of the children who are waiting for parents, but television can link only a small proportion of the waiting children with prospective families.

PLACEMENT THROUGH ADOPTION AGENCIES

Many adoption agencies have developed their own methods of finding homes for hard to place children. One agency that has been very active in this area is the Holt International Children's Services. This agency began about a quarter century ago with pioneering work in South Korea, placing many children of mixed race in Korean and American homes. Recently, Holt has placed as many as 3,000 children a year from Vietnam, Thailand, the Philippines, Nicaragua, and India, making it one of the largest agencies in the field of international adoptions. It also finds families for children born in the United States. Holt workers try to find parents for a child in his or her native country, but if none can be found, a family in another country is sought.

Holt reaches large numbers of would-be adoptive parents through its publication *HI Families,* which is sent to parents who have already adopted children from other countries through the agency. One page of this bulletin frequently includes pictures and descriptions of hard to place children. For example, 6-year-old Roberto is pictured with a patch over one eye and an expression that seems to ask for help. The details of his case explain that he is losing the sight in both eyes because of congenital glaucoma. Doctors in Nicaragua, where he lives, feel that his eyesight cannot be saved but that he would benefit from the love and caring of a family, and grow in every way. When asked about the patch on his eye, Roberto says, "A dog bite me." He is described as a small, attractive young boy who eats everything, though his appetite is small.

The Holt newsletter also features a double spread of pictures and descriptions of children under the headline "Have You a Home for One of These?" For example, Peter Gonzales is a 14-year-old boy from the Philippines whose chances of adoption will end soon because of his age. He will no longer be eligible for an orphan visa if someone does not choose to adopt him within months. He lives in an orphanage, where he is described as a good and obedient boy who acts as an older brother to the younger children. He does well in school and very much wants to belong to a family he can call his own. If Peter sounds like someone you might want to adopt, the newsletter explains, you can obtain more information about him and what you must do to qualify as an adoptive parent by contacting the agency.

Another famous adoption agency is the Tressler-Lutheran Service Associates of York, Pennsylvania. Early in the 1970's, this organization changed from placing healthy young white children to placing children with special needs. It concentrates on older children, over the age of 5, who are biracial, black, or from a foreign country. Many of this agency's children also have physical, emotional, or mental disabilities. Another class of children with special needs at Tressler is groups of brothers and sisters who hope to find a home all together. The agency once placed a family of seven brothers and sisters with adoptive parents.

Although a number of agencies concentrate on hard to place children or those with special needs, the Tressler agency prides itself on new approaches to helping these children. For example, the group home study process is a program of self-assessment by parents who are planning to adopt. Special emphasis is placed on using experienced adoptive parents to help those who are planning to adopt or who have adopted children within the past six months.

[61]

ADOPTING CHILDREN
WITH SPECIAL NEEDS:
THE PARENTS' VIEW

Families that share their experiences in adopting children with special needs are, perhaps, the best publicists for these children. They are able to tell the world about the challenges and the deep satisfactions of fulfilling the needs of the children they have adopted.

Dorothy and Bob DeBolt are probably the best known among those who have publicly shared their experiences. Through adoption and legal guardianship, they have added thirteen children to their biological family of six children, and eight of the thirteen have disabilities. Some of the DeBolts' adoptions have received national attention. Their adopted daughter Karen, for example, a black quadruple amputee, was featured in articles in two national magazines. The DeBolts are working to make the public aware that such children are not morbid, sad, or tragic, but can be beautiful, exciting, and vibrantly alive. The DeBolts' story is told in the book *19 Steps up the Mountain,* and they feel that their experiences will help to dispel the negative views of many people toward taking children with special needs. Their interest in hard to place children has also resulted in the development of an agency, Aid to Adoption of Special Kids, or AASK. The agency, which functions as a referral service, reports that their waiting lists contain as many as 2,000 families who want to adopt children with special needs.

The Chapmans are a family that has adopted children through AASK, as well as through Holt International Children's Services. Some years ago, after talking over the idea of adopting children with special needs with their five biological children, the Chapmans decided to adopt a handicapped child. They first took a boy who had suffered from polio and had been living at the Holt Orphanage in Korea for four years. He was considered so handicapped that no one had asked about him, but he had worked hard with a physical therapist, who helped him progress from a body brace and crawling on the floor to walking with crutches and braces. The therapist had told him that he might get a family if he worked hard on his program, and he did: when the Chapmans heard his story they started the adoption process immediately.

The second child the Chapmans adopted had lived in the streets of Seoul for two years before coming to the Holt Orphanage. He, too, had had polio and was fitted with a leg brace. A third child, who had also suffered from polio, was adopted by the family. The fourth boy was suggested to them by AASK because his first adoptive home had not worked out and the agency was worried about him. He was paralyzed from the chest down as a result of war injuries in South Korea. When he arrived at the Chapmans', this 6-year-old boy had never been in one place long enough to put down any roots or learn to trust anyone. Although there were problems at first, he grew to be a happy, outgoing person who is an inspiration to those around him. Another child added to the list of adoptees in this family was a girl whose main handicap was just being 13, an age when many people do not want to consider a girl for adoption.

Mrs. Chapman reports that these adopted children have opened up a new dimension for the family and given them something one could never buy. The individuals in this family are no longer afraid to talk about their problems—past, present, or future. Each one feels loved, wanted, and valued as a contributing member of the family.

LINKING PARENTS AND CHILDREN

Even though there are an increasing number of people adopting children with special needs, there are still many children who wait because they have not found parents who are willing to take them. A large step in helping such children was taken in October, 1979, when the federal government established the National Adoption Information Exchange System (NAIES) and contracted with the Child Welfare League to develop the program. This program established a national network to link children and parents. It replaces a similar program established by the League in 1968. Both programs have been an invaluable aid to agencies when they are unable to find a permanent home for a child locally.

NAIES publishes a newsletter, *Waiting Children,* which highlights many of the children who are listed on the exchange. The newsletter, which is published ten times a year, is available without charge upon request from The North American Center on Adoption, 67 Irving Place, New York, New York 10003. The Center also works with welfare professionals to provide training and consultation on special adoption issues and plays a key role in encouraging and drafting legislation that benefits both the children and the families they join by adoption.

Adoptive parent groups are also active in linking children with parents. There are about 500 adoptive parent groups in the United States with a wide variety of goals and orientations. The North American Council on Adoptable Children was founded in 1974 by members of some of these groups to serve as a national voice for families who are involved in adoptions. The council aims at coordinating and supporting the efforts of many volunteers who are interested in the welfare of children and the needs of parents. This organization has many programs, such as the publication of the journal *Adoptalk,* which focuses on adoption and parenting, and the national distribution of current printed materials on adoption and related subjects. The Council also sponsors a national week that increases awareness of children with special needs.

Another group that works actively for children's welfare is the National Association of Black Social Workers. This group believes that black homes can be found for black children, including those who are hard to place. They emphasize that children trapped in the child welfare system have other options than just a white adoptive home or a life of institutionalization. They believe there are enough black families willing and able to adopt children. The association recruits black adoptive homes, educates the black community about the plight of the black child in adoption, and works to change child care agency policies and state laws that make it difficult for black children to be adopted.

If you are interested in learning more about the work of groups or agencies, consult your local or state department of social services and some of the groups listed on pages 77 to 81. Even if you never plan to be part of a family that is involved in adoption, you can play a role in helping some of the children who wait.

CHAPTER
7
SEARCHING
FOR ROOTS

When John was 16 years old, he packed his bag and joined a friend to run away to the city where their adoption records were held. Everyone was talking about roots, but they knew nothing about theirs. Why shouldn't they know who their birth parents were?

For years, John had watched the faces of women he passed on the street. When he saw one whose nose or eyes resembled his, he wondered if she might be his mother. He was certain that his biological mother would be better than the one who had adopted him. Besides, he had a right to know who he was.

John and his friend had not gone far when they ran out of money and called home to their adoptive parents. But even if they had reached the government office where their adoption records were kept, they would not have been able to unlock the files, because all adoption records are sealed. This practice is intended to protect everyone involved in the adoption—the biological parents, the adoptive parents, and the child.

Traditionally, adoption has been like a rebirth for the child. At the time of the adoption proceedings, a new birth certificate is issued. The date and place of the child's actual birth remain the same, but the names of the biological parents are replaced by the names of the adoptive parents, just as if the new parents had given birth to the child. The legal relationship between the biological parent and the child is terminated. The adopted child grows up free of any stigma connected with the birth and without the need to deal with two sets of parents. The biological parents are free to live their lives without fear that any episode from the past might return to haunt them. And the adoptive parents may also feel free of any danger that the child will reject them in favor of the biological parents.

In recent years, however, changing attitudes have caused people to question the policy of sealing adoption records. For example, the attitude of many people toward illegitimacy has softened. New medical knowledge has shown many diseases and conditions to be hereditary, thereby increasing the importance of knowing about the health of one's ancestors. And emphasis on finding one's roots has added to the demand that adopted children have a legal right to learn the identity of their biological parents.

A natural outgrowth of this new awareness is the desire of adopted children to find their biological parents. Some adoptees search long and hard to find the mothers who gave them birth. Consider the case of Paul, who grew up in a family whose interests and temperament were different from his. For many years Paul had been curious about his background, but he did nothing about searching for his natural mother. He did not want to hurt his adoptive parents' feelings, but he felt that he just had to know more about his origin. Now that he was grown, he could search for information without causing suspicions about what he was doing.

A few months after he was married, Paul went to the courthouse of his native city and explained to the clerk that he was planning to have children. He wanted to know something about his medical background. The file on Paul's adoption revealed that there was nothing unusual in his medical history, and the clerk replaced it quickly as though he were hiding a great secret. Paul talked with the man about his desire to know more about his past, but the clerk would only reveal that his mother's name was Ann Robinson. He explained that he only gave Paul this information because his mother had moved away. Paul had already learned from his adoptive parents that his mother had moved to Chicago soon after he was born. So now he knew her name and where she might live. He also remembered that they had mentioned that she was a nurse.

With these leads, Paul flew to Chicago and checked the nurses' registries and the membership lists of every association that he thought might lead him to the location of a nurse named Ann Robinson. He found two nurses with that name, but both were far too young to have been his mother. Of course, she might have married and taken her husband's name.

After the disappointment of not finding his mother in Chicago, Paul decided to discuss the matter with his adoptive parents. Perhaps they would understand his feelings and help him in his search. One night after dinner, Paul brought up the subject by saying that he needed help in learning more about his medical history in the hope that it would alert him to any problems if he and his new wife had children. His mother became very uncomfortable, but his father promised to mail him a copy of all the medical information they were given when the adoption took place.

Paul watched for the mail day after day hoping that his father would provide some helpful details along with the medical history. He was right. When the neatly typed medical history arrived, there was a pencilled note telling Paul that his mother had married a man named Harod, a professor of chemistry at a university in Chicago. Now Paul could certainly find his mother. Suddenly he was frightened. Would she want to see him? How would he approach her? Perhaps she had divorced the professor and remarried. Perhaps he would never find her after all.

Paul waited for several months before following the leads that might answer many of the questions that had been gnawing at him for years. If his mother refused to see him, would he feel rejected again? He imagined many meetings with his mother, and finally he decided the truth would be better than imagining. He would actively continue to search for her.

The librarian at the local library helped him to find the name of a chemistry professor named Harod. He had transferred several times, but there was a listing for him in a recent directory in a city about 100 miles away. Paul was able to locate his residence and his home phone. Should he call and find out if a Mrs. Harod was there? Could he check through neighbors to find out if this professor had remarried or had been widowed? He decided to call and ask a few discreet questions. Through the call, he learned that he had a half-brother several years younger and a half-sister who was still in college. Their mother was flying to visit a friend in Paul's hometown the very next day. Without revealing his identity, he learned her flight number and arranged to board the same plane.

Paul sat in the airport waiting room, watching each woman who was taking the plane. He rejected one as too old, another as too young. He debated between the only two women who were possible candidates and wondered if he should approach one before boarding the plane. His heart was racing as he took a step toward the most likely woman. Her face was shaped like his and her chin had a similar cleft. Then the flight number was called, and people began boarding.

When everyone was settled on the plane, Paul was pleased to see that no one was sitting next to the woman who was probably the mother he had been wanting to meet for as long as he could remember. He moved to the seat next to her and exchanged small talk. Early in the flight, he asked questions about where she had lived, and established that this must be the woman who had placed him for adoption. Paul told this woman the story of his search for his mother, and he could see that she was beginning to wonder if this might be her son. When she realized the truth, she did not throw her arms around him as he had hoped, but grew cool and announced that she did not wish to discuss the matter. Before the flight was over, Paul had established that she did not want to interrupt her present life in any way. He could not explain what he really wanted from her, but they did exchange conversation about feelings that had been buried for a long time. When Paul said goodbye to her at the airport, he knew that he would

[71]

never see his mother again. But his search had ended, and he felt that he understood why she had made the decision to place him for adoption.

Some searches end in tearful embraces. Some end with the complete rejection of children by parents who wish they had never been found. Some searches never end.

Because the issue of sealed adoption records touches a great many people who have different interests at stake, it has become very controversial. Those who are involved feel very strongly on both sides of the issue. Some believe that records should be available to adults who have been adopted; others believe that they should not be.

One group that wants adoption records made available to those who ask is Concerned United Birthparents. Many biological parents of adopted children prefer to remain anonymous or even live in fear of discovery, but the parents in this organization want to locate the children they placed for adoption. Many biological parents state that they have never satisfactorily resolved their conflicting feelings about having given up their children. Some claim that they were pressured at a time in their lives when they did not know where to turn, and that they regretted the decision after signing the papers that released their children. Now some of these parents who felt guilt and shame when their children were born experience the same feelings at having given them up. They now hope to find the children so that they can explain the forces that compelled them to surrender them. In some cases, they might wish to establish relationships with the children.

On the adoptees' side of the issue, much of the attention has focused on the psychological effects of being denied access to information about the biological parents. Some psychiatrists state emphatically that not knowing the whole story of one's origin at an early age can hamper the proper development of an individual's identity. Further psychological damage can occur if an adoptee is later prevented from obtaining information about his or her biological parents. Among the organizations that favor open birth records are several that help adoptees who feel strong needs to know the truth about their backgrounds. Two of these organizations, Orphan Voyage and the Adoptees' Liberty Movement Association, also press for legislation to unseal adoption records.

Access to birth records might relieve adoptees and biological parents of weeks of sifting through dusty files, old telephone books, and registries, but does it really solve everyone's problems? Some adoptees are motivated by anger toward the biological parents. It is emotionally painful to learn that one was given away as a baby, and if this hurt is not acknowledged, it may be repressed and allowed to fester. Later these feelings may be translated into a burning desire to find one's roots. Many adoptees may have unconscious plans to make their parents feel guilty. Some psychiatrists and psychologists believe that the problems of adopted children could be better solved if they accepted the reasons for their impulse to search for roots, and found their fulfillment through loving others. At present, adoption records remain sealed in varying degrees in all states, and there is disagreement about the number of adopted adults who would really take advantage of a change in the law. In England, for example, the Children's Act of 1975 gave all adopted people over 18 years of age access to their birth records. Five years later the Department of Health and Social Services issued a report to Parliament in which it noted that the proportion of all adopted adults who took advantage of the legislation was less than expected. Only about 1 or 2 percent came forward for information about their original birth certificates. It is believed that even fewer traced their natural mothers, but those who did appear to have done so with discretion. For most of these people, the important factor was learning the truth, not the need for a happy reunion with a parent.

Dr. John Triseliotis, a Scottish psychiatrist and specialist in adoption problems, feels that the impulse to search is part of a deeply felt psychological need to obtain information that would help the adoptee feel more complete. He described it as a "tying up of loose ends." Adoptees who were generally satisfied with their home life were less interested in meeting their biological parents than those who had a poorer self-image or whose information about their adoption had been given in a hostile way.

On the other hand, Mrs. Margaret Mawer, the assistant director of the Association of British Adoption and Fostering Agencies, notes that there has been a rapid decline in children available for adoption since the passage of the Children's Act. She believes this fact may be partly due to the fear of biological mothers that access to birth records will mean that they may be traced later. A large survey in Los Angeles, California, however, indicated that only one third of the parents questioned would seek to avoid contact if they learned that the children they had given up for adoption were actively looking for them.

Certainly, each case of adoption differs, and the members of the adoption triangle—the adoptive parents, the biological parents, and the adoptee—must all be considered in the controversy over sealed records. The Association for the Protection of the Adoptive Triangle advocates the maintenance of comprehensive files on an adoptee's biological parents and their backgrounds, interests, and medical records. But the Association believes that the actual identities of these people should be withheld. At the other extreme are groups that believe all records should be available when an adopted person reaches the age of 18 or 21. In the United States the trend today appears to be toward more access for adoptees to information about their biological parents. Some adoption agencies will now share biographical data on biological parents. Some will even act as go-betweens, contacting the biological mother or father or both, informing them that the child wants to arrange a meeting, and telling them how to contact the child. One popular approach is the creation of a confidential file containing the names and addresses of adopted persons and biological parents who wish to meet each other or simply to exchange information. Adoption agencies use the list in acting as intermediaries to assist those who wish to communicate.

The agencies, however, encourage them to consider fully all the consequences if they do so. A clearinghouse such as this can also record statements from those who do not wish to be identified.

The controversy over sealed adoption records has arisen chiefly because the adult adoptees today were generally given up as babies. The changing nature of the adoption system, however, means that the adult adoptees of tomorrow will, in all likelihood, have quite a different attitude toward contacting their biological parents. Many of the adoptable children of the 1980's have been neglected, abandoned, or abused. The ties with their biological parents have been cut for very different reasons from those of the adoptees of twenty or thirty years ago. Most of today's adoptive parents will not experience the fear that adoptees who search for roots today create for some adoptive and biological parents.

FOR FURTHER INFORMATION

SPECIAL INTEREST GROUPS

Committee for Single Adoptive Parents
P. O. Box 4074
Washington, D.C. 20015

Child Welfare League of America, Inc. (CWLA)
National Adoption Information Exchange System (NAIES)
North American Center on Adoption
67 Irving Place
New York, New York 10003

Children's Defense Fund
1520 New Hampshire Avenue, N.W.
Washington, D.C. 20036

National Association of Black Social Workers (NABSW)
1969 Madison Avenue
New York, New York 10035

National Foster Parents Association (NFPA)
P. O. Box 16523
Clayton, Missouri 63105

North American Council on Adoptable Children
Information and Research Office
250 East Blair
Riverside, California 92507

North American Council on Adoptable Children
National Office
1346 Connecticut Avenue, N.W., Suite 229
Washington, D.C. 20036

Organization of Foster Families for Equality and Reform
P. O. Box 110
East Meadow, New York 11554

SOME AGENCIES THAT SPECIALIZE IN CHILDREN WITH SPECIAL NEEDS

*AASK—Aid to Adoption of Special Kids
3530 Grand Avenue
Oakland, California 94610

The Adoption of Special Children
Medina Children's Services
123 16th Avenue
Seattle, Washington 98122

Child Care Association of Illinois
2101 West Lawrence Avenue
Springfield, Illinois 62704

Children's Adoption Resource Exchange
1039 Evarts Street, N.W.
Washington, D.C. 20017

Children's Home Society of California
5429 McConnell Avenue
Los Angeles, California 90066

Children Unlimited, Inc.
P. O. Box 11463
Columbia, South Carolina 29211

Council of Adoptive Parents (CAP)
33 South Washington Street
Rochester, New York 14608

Delaware Valley Adoption Resource Exchange
1218 Chestnut Street, Suite 204
Philadelphia, Pennsylvania 19107

Dillon Family and Youth Services
2525 East 21st Street
Tulsa, Oklahoma 74102

*†New York Spaulding for Children
19 West 44th Street
New York, New York 10036

Northwest Adoption Exchange
P. O. Box 2526
Boise, Idaho 83701

*Pierce-Warwick Adoption Service
5229 Connecticut Avenue N.W.
Washington, D.C. 22215

Project CAN
2960 Roosevelt Boulevard
Clearwater, Florida 35520

Rocky Mountain Adoption Resource Exchange
El Paso County D. S. S.
105 North Spruce Street
Colorado Springs, Colorado 80905

Services to Unmarried Mothers and Adoption (SUMA)
1216 East McMillan Street
Cincinnati, Ohio 45206

*†Spaulding for Children—Michigan
3660 Waborus Road
Chelsea, Michigan 48118

†*Spaulding for Children has many branches. Write this
agency to see if there is a branch closer to your home.*

Specialized Adoption Resource Center
7100 West 44th Avenue, Suite 208
Wheat Ridge, Colorado 80033

Special Needs Adoption Program
Lutheran Social Services
1855 North Hillside Avenue
Wichita, Kansas 67214

*Tressler-Lutheran Service Associates
25 West Springettsbury Avenue
York, Pennsylvania 17403

SOME AGENCIES THAT SPECIALIZE IN INTERNATIONAL ADOPTIONS

Concerned Persons for Adoptions
200 Parsippany Road
Whippany, New Jersey 07981

Crossroads
4901 West 77th Street
124B
Minneapolis, Minnesota 55435

David Livingstone Missionary Foundation
Adoption Program
P. O. Box 232
Tulsa, Oklahoma 74101

Families for Children, Inc.
10 Bowling Green
Pointe Claire, 720
Quebec, Canada

FANA
Calle 71A
5-67
Bogotá, Colombia

*Especially well known

Foreign Adoption Center, Inc. (FAC)
2701 Alcott Street, Suite 471
Denver, Colorado 80211

Fundación Los Pisingos
Carrera 1 #68–79
Bogotá, Colombia

Kuan-Yin Foundation, Inc.
R. R. #1 Burlington
Ontario, Canada

Holt Adoption Program, Inc.
P. O. Box 2440
Eugene, Oregon 97402

International Adoptions, Inc.
218 Walnut Street
Newton, Massachusetts 02160

Latin America Parents Association (LAPA)
P. O. Box 72
Seaford, New York 11783

Missionaries of Charity, Mrs. Kathy Streedhar
2562 36th Street N.W.
Washington, D.C. 20007

Love the Children
221 West Broad Street
Quakertown, Pennsylvania 18954

Organization for a United Response, Inc. (OURS)
4711 30th Avenue South
Minneapolis, Minnesota 55406

Welcome House
P. O. Box 836
Doylestown, Pennsylvania 18901

World Family Adoptions, Ltd.
5048 Fairy Chasm Road
West Bend, Wisconsin 53091

GROUPS INTERESTED IN SEARCHING
FOR BIOLOGICAL PARENTS

Adoptees in Search
4304 Stanford Street
Chevy Chase, Maryland 20015

Adoptees' Liberty Movement Association (ALMA)
P.O. Box 154
Washington Bridge Station
New York, New York 10033

Orphan Voyage
R. D. #1, Box 153A
Cedaredge, Colorado 81413

Parent Finders
1408 West 45th Avenue
Vancouver, British Columbia V3B 1N7
Canada

GROUP INTERESTED IN SEARCHING
FOR BIOLOGICAL CHILDREN

Concerned United Birthparents, Inc. (CUB)
P. O. Box 753
Milford, Massachusetts 01757

SUGGESTIONS FOR FURTHER READING

American Public Welfare Association, *Intercountry Adoption Guidelines*. Washington, D.C.: Government Printing Office, 1980

American Public Welfare Association, *National Directory of Intercountry Adoption Service Resources*. Washington, D.C.: Government Printing Office, 1980

Beatty, Patricia, *That's One Ornery Orphan*. New York: William Morrow and Company, 1980

Benet, Mary Kathleen, *The Politics of Adoption*. New York: The Free Press, 1976

Berman, Claire, *We Take This Child: A Candid Look at Modern Adoption*. Garden City, New York: Doubleday and Company, 1974

Blank, Joseph P., *19 Steps up the Mountain: The Story of the DeBolt Family*. Philadelphia: J. P. Lippincott, 1976

Bunin, Sherry and Catherine, *Is That Your Sister?* New York: Pantheon Books, 1976

Burgess, Linda Cannon, *The Art of Adoption*. Washington, D.C.: Acropolis Books, 1976

Fanshel, David, and Eugene Shinn, *Children in Foster Care: A Longitudinal Investigation*. New York: Columbia University Press, 1978

Felker, Evelyn H., *Foster Parenting Young Children: Guidelines from a Foster Parent.* New York: Child Welfare League, 1974

Fisher, Florence, *The Search for Anna Fisher.* New York: Fawcett, 1977

Geiser, Robert L., *Illusion of Caring: Children in Foster Care.* Boston: Beacon Press, 1973

Goldstein, Joseph, Anna Freud, and Albert J. Solnit, *Before the Best Interests of the Child.* New York: The Free Press, 1979

Goldstein, Joseph, Anna Freud, and Albert J. Solnit, *Beyond the Best Interests of the Child.* New York: The Free Press, 1973

Grow, Lucille J., and Deborah Shapiro, *Transracial Adoption Today: Views of Adoptive Parents and Social Workers.* New York: Child Welfare League, 1975

Hyde, Margaret O., *Cry Softly: The Story of Child Abuse.* Philadelphia: Westminster Press, 1980

Jewett, Claudia L., *Adopting the Older Child.* Cambridge, Massachusetts: The Harvard Common Press, 1978

Kline, Draza, and Helen-Mary F. Overstreet, *Foster Care of Children: Nurture and Treatment.* New York: Columbia University Press, 1972

Kravik, Patricia J., ed., *Adopting Children with Special Needs.* Washington, D.C.: Colophon Press, 1977

Lasnick, R. S., *A Parents' Guide to Adoption.* New York: Sterling Publishing Company, 1979

Lifton, Betty Jean, *Lost and Found: The Adoption Experience.* New York: Dial Press, 1979

Lifton, Betty Jean, *Twice Born: Memoirs of an Adopted Daughter.* New York: McGraw-Hill, 1975

McNamara, Joan, *The Adoption Advisor.* New York: Hawthorn Books, 1975

Martin, Cynthia D., *Beating the Adoption Game.* San Diego, California: Oak Tree Publications, 1980

Meezan, William, Sanford Katz, and Eva Manoff Russo, *Adoptions without Agencies.* New York: Child Welfare League, 1978

[84]

Nelson-Erichsen, Jean, and Heins R. Erichsen, *How to Adopt Internationally*. Winona, Minn.: St. Mary's College, 1980

Rutter, Barbara A., *A Way of Caring: The Parents' Guide to Foster Family Care*. New York: Child Welfare League 1978

Sorosky, Arthur D., Annette Baran, and Reuben Pannor, *The Adoption Triangle: The Effects of the Sealed Record on Adoptees, Birth Parents, and Adoptive Parents*. New York: Anchor Press, 1978

INDEX

Friday's Child (Philadelphia), 60
Funding, lack of, 8
Further information listings, 77–82

"Gold-plated babies," 56, 59
Government financial assistance to families that adopt handicapped children, 59
Government relief for child care, early, 13
Government's involvement in foster care, 44–45
"Gray" market adoptions, 51, 52
Groups interested in searching for biological children (list), 82
Groups interested in searching for biological parents (list), 82

Henry VIII, laws affecting children, 14
HI Families, 60
Holt International Children's Services, 60, 62–63
Homebuilder therapists, 35–36

Indentured children, 14, 15–16
Information listings, 77–82
Institute for Child Advocacy (Ohio), 45

Juvenile court, 4

Linking parents and children, 63
Long-term foster care, 5
cost of, 36

Mawer, Margaret, 74
Mental health services, 8
Middle Ages, child care in, 12–13
Misconceptions about placement in foster homes, children's, 23

National Adoption Information Exchange System (NAIES), 63–64
National Association of Black Social Workers, 64–65
National Commission on Children in Need of Parents, 31
New York Asylum for Idiots, 17
New York Juvenile Asylum, 17
19 Steps up the Mountain, 62
North American Center on Adoption, 64

Oregon Project, 38
Orphanages, first, 16–17
Orphan Voyage, 73
Out-of-state placement, 30, 31